THE ESSENCE OF TEAMWORK

THE ESSENCE

OF TEAMWORK

ALMON GUNTER

HIGHLY ACCLAIMED SPEAKER & CONSULTANT

SPEED, STRENGTH, & CONDITIONING COACH

LIFE COACH

FOREWORD BY ERIC BASS

CO FOUNDER OF MOTIVATIONAL COACHING AND TRAINING SYSTEMS (MOCATS)

The Essence of Teamwork

Copyright © 2022 AGE 3, LLC

Print Edition   ISBN - 979-8-218-00081-3

All rights reserved. No portion of this book may be reproduced, stored in a retrieval system, or transmitted in any form or by any means—electronic, mechanical photocopy, recording, or any other—except for brief quotations in printed reviews without prior permission from AGE 3, LLC.

Printed in the United States of America.

For information or to request authorization to make copies of any part of this work contact:

AGE 3, LLC
Post Office Box 194
Jacksonville, Florida 32234
Office Phone 904.803.1917
Web Address: www.almongunterexperience.com
Email: almon@almongunterexperience.com

Twitter: @almongunter
Facebook: Almon Gunter Experience
LinkedIn: Almon Gunter
Instagram: Almon Gunter Experience
YouTube: Almon Gunter Experience
Podcast: Almon Gunter Experience
TikTok: @almongunterexperience

DEDICATION

This book is dedicated to the many parents, coaches, and leaders who put in countless hours bringing individuals together for common goals and to those who strive to live the philosophy "Together Everyone Achieves More Successfully" (TEAMS).

CONTENTS

Foreword	5
Introduction	7
Chapter 1: People of Character	15
Chapter 2: Outstanding Leadership	27
Chapter 3: Trust and Respect	39
Chapter 4: Outstanding Talent	49
Chapter 5: Committed	59
Chapter 6: Passionate	67
Chapter 7: Empower Each Other	79
Chapter 8: Think Team	87
Summary	97
About the Author	103
Acknowledgments	105

FOREWORD

The importance of teamwork is one of the hardest things an individual learns. How do you put the interest of the group before yourself and understand how this will help you the most in the end? It is human nature for most people to say to themselves: "I must take care of myself first. What is best for me?" The hardest thing for coaches or corporate leaders to do is to get the members of their organizations to work together as a team. Individuals must learn to forget about what they will achieve on their own and instead to focus on, "What can we achieve together?" How do leaders get their charges to fight for the person next to them as hard as they would fight for themselves or their families? This is not an easy task, yet it can be done. In this book, Almon Gunter shows leaders how to get individuals to think and act as a team.

Almon Gunter, in *The Essence of Teamwork*, has laid out a clear, wonderful program showing leaders and their members how to become architects of strong, successful teams. This book is a must-read for all who aspire to have successful careers in the worlds of business, athletics, education, or any of life's many endeavors. Almon Gunter is giving you the essential points for building a winning team.

Eric Bass
Co-Founder of MOCATS

INTRODUCTION

Teamwork is defined by Merriam-Webster's unabridged dictionary as "work done by a number of associates with usually each doing a clearly defined portion but all subordinating personal prominence to the efficiency of the whole" to achieve a specific task. The definition sounds easy enough, but actually bringing a group of people together to achieve a specific task is a whole different ball game (no pun intended). The word "teamwork" is used everywhere—from families in their homes, to corporate entities, to actual sports teams. While we hear the word constantly, the real issue is that most people don't understand what it actually means to be a part of a team or how to work together for a common goal. In other words, it is very hard to "walk the talk" every day, especially for those who have never been trained to be effective members of an effective team.

    Some of you may be familiar with the phrase, "walk the walk"; that is, to act in ways that show others you do what you say you believe. A newer expression, "walk the talk," means that you act on your beliefs (walk the walk), AND you follow through to accomplish what you promise to yourself and others you will accomplish every day—PLUS you support your teammates in their efforts to walk the talk. Walking the walk is difficult, but walking the talk is even more demanding. This book is going to teach you how to be a team leader and simultaneously a team member: not only how to walk the talk, but also how to become totally committed to doing it as a central part of your life.

When you really stop to think about it, probably only 10 percent of the population ever participated on a varsity level sports team in high school. Regardless of the total student population of the school, only about 10 percent of the student body takes part in school athletics. Actually, the smaller the school, the more you will find that most student athletes were multiple sport athletes. I am not saying that you must have participated in a team sport at a varsity level to understand teamwork, but it certainly helps.

When I speak in a corporate environment, I always ask the question, "How many of you in this room played a varsity level sport in high school?" The number always comes out to about 10 percent of the people in the room. However, if my talk is for a sales group or a sales team, the percentage of individuals who participated in high school athletics increases. Usually, salespeople were athletes or are very sports minded. That makes sense when you look at the characteristics of a successful salesperson. Athletics demand focus, discipline, drive, aggression, confidence, and a can-do attitude, which are the same characteristics business managers look for in good salespeople. Also, I've repeatedly learned that upper management's directors, vice presidents, presidents, and chief executive officers more times than not were associated with or participated in sports on some level. So naturally, most organizations talk about teamwork and working together to achieve organizational goals, but, unfortunately, the majority of people in the workforce struggle to understand the true concept of teamwork.

In professional football, the concept of only going 30 feet to pick up a first down may seem like no big deal, but within that

30 feet are 22 bodies, ranging from 175 lbs. to 330+ lbs., 11 trying to get the 30 feet and 11 trying to stop the other team from gaining the 30 feet. That is a lot of competition, and these players are the best of the best. The same can be said about professional basketball, professional baseball, professional hockey, professional tennis, professional golf, and professional track and field. These are the best of the best competing at levels that most people cannot comprehend or even dream about. So, the concept of a professional team playing together to achieve one goal is extremely different from being a member or leader of a typical business organization.

Yet this is where I say we should all aspire to work together to achieve whatever our goals are, just as a professional sport team does. Our families should have specific goals that are tangible and measurable, and the goals we set for our families collectively and individually should be reviewed weekly. We should evaluate our plays and the execution of our plays, that is, our division of labor and the quality of time we spend together and apart, on a regular basis to make sure we are maximizing our potential as a family unit. Corporate entities should also evaluate their plays the same way. The average corporate entity will set goals for the year but will not review or evaluate where they are in reference to hitting those goals until three months or six months have passed or at the year's end. This is not a recipe for success; this is a recipe for disaster. Can you imagine what would happen to professional sports teams if they operated this way? Professional teams know at all times what they are playing for. They know who their competition is, they know what their competition is doing (they study films of their opponents), each athlete's role is clearly defined, and each person's expectations are clear and concise. Everyone knows what is at stake, and there are no surprises about where the team stands or how it stacks up to its competition from week to week.

Great teams operate with the motto "Right Is Right." Everyone is on the same page—no ifs, ands, or buts about it. They make sure that all team members know the team's goal and know their roles and responsibilities within achieving that goal. It is important that every team member knows how he or she fits within the organization. It is also important to make sure that personal and team goals are aligned to give the team the best chance to win. Teamwork is more than talk. It is more than two or more people working together or getting along. Teamwork is everyone—including the players, coaches, trainers, drivers, physicians, and all staff members—doing "whatever it takes" to maximize the potential of every other person on the team.

This book, *The Essence of Teamwork*, outlines the eight qualities all great teams demonstrate consistently that set them apart from the rest. Each of these characteristics provides a necessary piece of the puzzle for overall success of the team. The following are the eight Characteristics of Teamwork:

1. People of Character. Individuals who are compelled to do what they say they will do are people with high moral values. It is important to have a group of individuals who hold themselves as well as everyone else on the team accountable for meeting and exceeding team goals. I call people like this *Super Freaks*—outstanding people who become outstanding members of a team or organization. We play with the perspective that there is enough for everyone if we each just do our part.

Teamwork is understanding that together we can and will achieve so much more than we can individually. (For a complete explanation of what it means to be a Super Freak and why I first created this designation for myself, check out Chapter 6 in this book.)

"Nearly all men can stand adversity, but if you want to test a man's character, give him power." Abraham Lincoln, 16th U.S. president

2. Outstanding Leadership. Great teams have incredible leaders. Outstanding leadership has nothing to do with having all the answers. Outstanding leadership is being competent and inspiring others to soar to heights they would never have achieved on their own. Outstanding leaders provide a constant source of motivation for those they lead; they are role models of the qualities and values they require of their team members. Leadership is being a visionary and knowing how to communicate vision in such a manner that everyone buys into the vision and is inspired to follow.

"People of action have high self-esteem, confidence, intelligence, egoism, and pride. And all of these characteristics will be regarded as extraordinary features if they use them to achieve great things. It ain't bragging if you can do it." Almon W. Gunter, Jr., author, coach, motivational speaker, and author of this book

Note: "Egoism" means believing that enlightened self-interest is at the root of moral conduct. That is, by acting to advance the interests of the team (or group) as a whole, each individual on the team also advances his or her own self-interest. In contrast, "egotism" is an exaggerated sense of one's own importance, shown by people who act as if they are superior to others. The distinction between these two words relates directly to the definition of teamwork: When team members subordinate (make less important) their own personal prominence (greatness) to ensure the efficiency of the whole team, they are working together to create the best possible team.

3. Trust and Respect. As a member of any team, you must trust and respect the people you are playing with. If you doubt that they will come through for you or think they will not be there for you when the going gets tough, you may as well pack it all in. Super Freaks trust and respect ourselves to deliver; therefore, we trust and respect others on our team, knowing that they will deliver as well. Trust and respect are built on facts, not emotion, so everyone can win.

"The most important elements of any relationship are trust and respect. When you trust someone enough to be honest with them, you grow to respect them and yourself. Where there [are] trust and respect, progress resides." Ritu Ghatourey, a poet and writer from India

4. Outstanding Talent. Teams that excel have outstanding talent. However, please note that I didn't say the best talent or exceptional talent. I said outstanding talent, meaning they have individuals who are coachable. Super Freaks have coachable talent. We are willing to learn, we listen well, we pay close attention, and we do the work. That is a winning combination all the way around. Talent that works hard every day to progress is essential for any successful team.

"Talent without discipline is like an octopus on roller skates. There is plenty of movement, but you never know if it is going to be forward, backwards, or sideways." H. Jackson Brown, Jr., author of Life's Little Instruction Book

5. Commitment. Super Freaks are committed to being the best. This is our only option. Failure is not an option. We operate with our backs against the wall, and we are wholeheartedly committed. When your back is against the wall, everything has to come toward you. The lack of options produces focus! Commitment means total dedication to a goal, not allowing any other options but doing what it takes to meet the goal.

"There are only two options regarding commitment: You're either in, or you're out. There is no such thing as life in between." Almon W. Gunter, Jr.

6. Passionate. Great teams are full of people who love what they do. They want to be a part of the team. They are full of life and energy, and they come to play every day. Super Freaks sum passion up this way: enthus**iasm** (**I A**m **S**old **M**yself)! Being passionate about what you do ensures that every day the game of life gets the very best you have to offer.

"Passion is energy. Feel the power that comes from focusing on what excites you." Oprah Winfrey, talk show host, media proprietor, and actress

7. Empowerment. This term simply means to let go. If you are truly a part of a team, you allow others to do what they were hired to do, and you do what you were brought on to do. It doesn't matter whether it's work, family, or sports. We all have a role to play, and we should be allowed to play it with proper leadership and guidance.

"Confidence and empowerment are cousins in my opinion. Empowerment comes from within, and typically it's stemmed and fostered by self-assurance. To feel empowered is to feel free and that's when people do their best work. You can't fake confidence or empowerment." Amy Jo Martin, founder of Digital Royalty and author

8. Think Team. It's never "I" or "me"; it's always "we." The Super Freak Way wants everyone to reach his or her full potential, whatever that potential may be. To do so requires thinking as a team member. The motto here is simple: All for one and one for all.

"The strength of the team is each individual member. The strength of each member is the team." Phil Jackson, pro basketball executive, former coach, and former player

As you read the following pages, as always, read with an open heart and open mind. Look within yourself because success is always an inside job. My sincere hope is that within this book you will find the information to be both inspiring and motivating so you can create and be a part of a winning team. Enjoy another journey as we once again ride together on the A–Train!

CHAPTER 1

People of Character

People of Character. *Individuals who are compelled to do what they say they will do are people of character, people who have high moral standards. It is important that a team is a group of individuals who hold themselves and everyone else on the team accountable for meeting and exceeding the team's goals. Super Freaks play with the perspective that there is enough for everyone if we each just do our part. Teamwork is understanding that together we can and will achieve so much more than we can individually. "Nearly all men can stand adversity, but if you want to test a man's character, give him power." Abraham Lincoln*

Great teams start with the people who are on the team. Every family, team, and organization are only as good as its people. The character of each individual on the team speaks volumes about what will and won't get done toward striving to achieve the personal, family, and professional goals of the team. So, let's start from the beginning. What does the word "character" mean? In Greek, character translates as "an enduring or indelible mark." Thus, character might be best defined as "values in action, the qualities that make up someone's personality, or the qualities that clearly make someone different from someone else. Abigail Van Buren, in her newspaper advice column, titled "Dear Abby," once wrote this regarding character:

"The best index to a person's character is (a) how he or she treats people who can't do him or her any good, and (b) how he or she treats people who can't fight back."

And my personal favorite regarding character is a quote from Colin Powell, retired four-star general in the U.S. Army and 65th U.S. Secretary of State: "If you want to see a person's character, just give him or her power."

People of character separate themselves from the pack by doing what they say they will do. Doing what you say you will do is an essential quality for teams if they are to succeed consistently. People of character are in no way, shape, or form perfect people. They are people who, whether they are right, wrong, or indifferent, will stand accountable for the consequences of their decisions. They don't point fingers to blame others, and their expectations of others are what they expect of themselves. People of character know that with every choice that is made, consequences follow. And the consequences that follow are directly related to the choices that are made. As individuals, all too many times we feel shocked by the consequences of certain choices we've made, when the truth is we knew going in what price we would pay for the choices we made. The Super Freak Way knows that there are no perfect people, but there are perfect teams. To achieve perfection as a team, all team members, coaches, and staff must be people of character.

As individuals and team members, people of character have a cluster of core values that they consistently put into action. Great character isn't a result of luck or erratic behavior. Instead, it is evident when our actions and thoughts are intentionally, freely, logically, and consistently chosen, including when we compete against other teams or individuals. Character is a collection of related processes, such as displaying honesty, respect, perseverance, and/or courage at all times.

The Super Freak Way demonstrates that character develops over time. Like most things in life that are worth having, becoming a person of character requires time, patience, and persistence. As I was growing up, my mother's philosophy was that her children would grow up to be who we wanted to be every day—the sooner the better. The sooner we teach our colleagues and teammates to celebrate what we want to see more of, the better off we and they are going to be as a team. How do we teach strength of character? We teach it by our own examples, by being role models. My mother also stressed the importance of patience. I can recall her telling me during my teenage years that all my prayers should be asking for patience. I guess you could say, like most people, I wanted everything NOW! I did pray for patience, and over time I received it in abundance. Sometimes I think I am too patient, but I will gladly accept this criticism, because in my life I have found that lack of patience led me to make stupid decisions. I learned that in order to be successful and achieve the goals that I had set for myself, I needed to develop character, to demonstrate a strong work ethic, commitment, efficiency, perseverance, and stay motivated and compete.

Character, like every other thing in life that has stood the test of time, can only last if it is built on a strong foundation. No one can say for certain how much character we develop in our early years; however, it is safe to say that character does not change quickly. A person's behavior is an indication of a person's character. Is the behavior weak, strong, good, or bad? Strong character is shown by high energy, self-determination, willpower, and a can-do attitude. We know that various factors shape our character, such as our family and school environments, our role models, socioeconomic status, as well as predispositions and talents we've inherited from our parents. These factors help shape the moral character in each of us. As children, we start to develop concern for others, a sense of justice, and integrity. We become conscious of social pressures and develop problem-solving and leadership skills. These factors of environment and heredity also influence how we develop a healthy life-style, life goals, self-discipline, and self-control, while we are committed to staying the course to achieve our goals.

People of character take responsibility for living the lives they want. They hold themselves accountable for doing whatever it takes to compete and be successful, both as individuals and as team members. As Super Freaks, we understand that using substandard building materials or cutting corners to build the lives we want will only lead to reworking and disappointment. If our life foundations aren't solid, the price we will pay to restore, remodel, and rebuild ourselves will be very costly. In the end, successful teams excel at designing, maintaining, and building upon a strong foundation. Team leaders and members expect the best from themselves and every individual on the team. People of character focus on developing knowledge, understanding specific social and mental skills, building commitment, and practicing good habits for living out their core values.

I understand that our world is constantly changing. The excuses I hear most often for not accomplishing goals are "This is how it is nowadays." Or, "Everything is so instant." Well, that may be the case, but success is built on patience, persistence, hard work, and time. The Super Freak Way is to build a legacy that will benefit many generations, and to do so it takes uncompromising character. When I research successful people or successful teams, the one key ingredient that always stands out is that they were and are people of character. They never compromise on quality, they are extremely patient, and they work harder and more efficiently than everyone else or than all the other teams.

The foundation for character, just as for many of the things needed to compete and win in the game of life, starts at home. I know that for many, strong support just doesn't happen at home; however, as a Super Freak, I believe that exposure to great role models when we are away from home can be even more important. For example, individuals we admire in the schools we attend, the organizations where we work, and the communities where we live can shape and influence our character every day. Ultimately, as individuals we are responsible for who and what we are. In addition to our families, our culture, community, and faith play key roles in how we develop as persons of character.

Great teams embrace the philosophy that everyone is important on the team and each person plays a key role in the overall success of the team. The best way to sum this up is that great teams live the African proverb: "It takes a village to raise a child." Teams that constantly excel rely on an endless supply of individuals who model the way for others to live. People of character are advocates for modeling, enforcing, teaching, and building a strong foundation for the success of the team.

As I was growing up, I was fortunate to have great role models all around me to help me stay my course. In addition to being an excellent role model himself, my grandfather reminded me constantly that the library was full of great role models. I read about people who made a difference, whose inventions and accomplishments made the world a better place for everyone, including Booker T. Washington, Frederick Douglass, Maya Angelou, Abraham Lincoln, Jesse Owens, Ida B Wells an Fannie Lou Hamer. These great people became my heroes. As I comprehended how they persevered in spite of adversity, sacrificed immediate gratification to accomplish long-term goals, and stayed committed to living out their dreams, I began to understand the real keys to success.

Great teams act on the theory that character development works best when it is "caught and taught." This simply means that parents, coaches, mentors, and leaders model the behavior they want to nurture and simultaneously label the actions and virtues they display. This process integrates the expectations of the community and lived experiences of leaders. Modeling expected behaviors while naming those behaviors is the most effective way to teach. Information is the game plan for freedom!

I was fortunate to have several great coaches in my life, but one coach stands out like no other. His name is Claude Simmons. "Coachy," as we referred to him, was my football and track coach from 7th through 12th grades. He by far provided the greatest inspiration for student athletes I have ever met. I remember that at the start of my senior year in high school, I wasn't going to play football. Coachy showed up at my house the first day of football practices (two a day). He talked to me, put me in his car, and took me to practice. He wasn't going to let me quit and gave me a laundry list of reasons why it was important that I played football my senior year. He was so right. It turned out that I had a great season and made all-everything my senior year. Coachy always modeled the behavior he expected of his student athletes. He never said one swear word, never got rattled, and just kept pushing forward. As a result of his leadership, our track team won the conference six consecutive years and won the district championship my senior year. You are probably thinking, "So what?" Right? Well, we won all of those titles, and we didn't have a track to train on! We ran on the road and around a softball field. So from 7th through 12th grades I was a champion. Learning how to win then has served me well throughout my career. Football Coach Vince Lombardi said, "Winning is a habit, but unfortunately so is losing." I am so grateful I learned how to win. Coachy taught us the values of hard work, focus, commitment, and patience. So I went from having no track to practice on to having the privilege of running in seven Olympic Stadiums globally and representing the United States of America in track. Not too shabby. What an incredible mentor and role model I had! Thanks, Coachy, for your words of encouragement, but even more important, thanks for walking the talk.

People of character have a sense of process, purpose, and structure. They share an interest in the process of building a strong foundation, as well as reaching the best outcome. Another way of saying this is people of character work together to get the desired results for everyone. They are flexible in their approach to achieving and have the abilities to adapt to any situation. The Super Freak Way is to focus on a shared vision that the team believes in and works to enact. It is easier to stay motivated when you believe in the process, help to create a foundation that can support any structure, and know your purpose within the team. In general, the most successful teams have a strong sense of community. This doesn't suggest that all the team members hang out together during their free time. It simply means that team members know and accept their roles and see the importance of each person. All team members share a strong sense of community: We know we are needed, valued, and supported. All team members or employees feel important, confident that no favoritism is shown for a select few.

People of character develop through healthy competition. They know they can only achieve their best when they challenge and support each other. As Super Freaks, we understand that in life we compete with each other, not against each other. An example of this: If you and I compete in the Olympics, and you win the gold medal but I set a personal record in that same race, your effort helped push me to achieve my best effort. I didn't win the gold, but I did do better than I had ever done before, so we both won.

People of character feel as responsible for the growth of their teammates as they do for their own development because when everyone in the community is strong, individuals as well as the team excel. At every level of competition, new levels of excellence are achieved when participants find good competitors. People of character come to understand that competition is "striving with" our teammates and our competitors instead of "striving against" them. By coming to this understanding, we appreciate, value, and even seek out competitors who will help get the best out of us. As well-matched competitors, Muhammad Ali and Joe Frazier, Magic Johnson and Larry Bird, Chris Evert and Martina Navratilova—all made each other better. By competing with each other, they forced each other to be better.

In an interview by NPR's Michele Norris, discussing the rivalry between Magic Johnson and himself, Larry Bird said,

"We did it in a way where we caught the imagination of everyone in America. People wanted to see us play against one another. . . . If you like competition you want to play against the best, and that's what we wanted to do" (To listen to or read the entire interview, go to www.npr.org/templates/story/story.php?storyId=120053152).

The Super Freak Way is always to take a common-sense approach to the game of life. After all, there is nothing new under the sun, right? Building a strong foundation for character is as simple as applying the **ABE** (**A**ttitude, **B**ehavior, and **E**ffort) principle: Attitude, Behavior, and Effort are elements that every individual gets to control. Each and every day we get to decide what our attitude will be. A very long time ago, my grandfather taught me that attitude only came in two flavors: good or bad. There is no in-between. When we wake up each morning, we get to choose what our attitude for the day will be. As People of

Character, we focus on maintaining a positive attitude—no matter what circumstances, obstacles, or opportunities we encounter each day.

Behavior, like attitude, comes in only two flavors. We all get to choose to behave well or badly. Most of us know the right things to do, but doing them consistently requires concentration and self-discipline. Conducting ourselves in the appropriate ways 24/7 requires 100-percent focus and never taking a play off. And finally, effort: People of Character are always committed to working as hard as they can for the good of the team. Super Freaks commit to giving 100-percent effort to doing the work over and over and over again without fail. Great teams succeed because of repetition. All team members have a positive *attitude*, show respect for others and themselves in their *behavior*, and make an all-out *effort* to do things right every day.

Maintaining our best Attitudes, Behaviors, and Efforts will shape our characters. When we nurture these three ingredients together, we will start the lifelong practice of building a strong foundation of character. Great teams cannot win consistently without People of Character. They cannot and will not leave a legacy of hope and achievement if People of Character are not on the team. The Super Freak Way recognizes that People of Character form the foundation upon which all great teams are built. To achieve the remaining seven principles of teamwork, we must be People of Character ourselves and raise all team members to the high standards of Attitude, Behavior, and Effort.

Scribbles and Doodles

Do you do what you say you will do? (Explain why or why not.)

_____
_____
_____
_____
_____
_____
_____
_____
_____
_____

List 3 things you do to assure you maintain a solid foundation for your character.

_____
_____
_____
_____
_____
_____
_____
_____
_____
_____

How have you or will you apply the ABE principle (**A**ttitude, **Be**havior, and **E**ffort) to your life?

_____
_____
_____
_____
_____
_____
_____
_____
_____
_____
_____
_____
_____

Final Thoughts:

_____
_____
_____
_____
_____
_____
_____
_____
_____
_____
_____
_____
_____

CHAPTER 2

Outstanding Leadership

Outstanding Leadership *is a must for a successful team. Great leadership comprises several different characteristics, and in this chapter, we will explore seven of the key components for being an outstanding leader.* Outstanding leaders have *vision, communicate their vision, have people skills, are people of character, are competent, are bold,* and *are servants to others.*

The first key component of outstanding leadership is *Vision.* The Super Freak Way recognizes that being a visionary is essential if you are going to lead people. It doesn't matter whether you are leading your family, friends, sports team, or organization. A great vision for how to move the group forward toward achieving the vision is a must. Being a visionary requires you to have a sense of mission and purpose and to believe in the art of conveying your invisible vision to your team. The best leaders have the ability to start with the end point (the vision) in mind and work backwards step by step.

When you examine the stories of great leaders of people, such as Walt Disney, Steve Jobs, Bill Gates, Coach John

Wooden, Oprah Winfrey, Dr. Martin Luther King, and Coco Chanel, what you find is that these individuals are or were incredible visionaries. Each one had the ability to see the future of an art, a technology, a team, or a movement when most others couldn't. These leaders had the courage to dedicate themselves to their invisible goals no matter the cost. This type of courage is what allowed these individuals to become outstanding leaders. The Super Freak Way to outstanding leadership is having the courage to dream dreams and take risks that few will dare to act upon. Leaders know what they are playing for and can visualize the end result, believing that the risks are worth taking.

The second key component to outstanding leadership is having the ability to *Communicate Your Vision*. Having a great vision for change, opportunity, and growth is all for nothing if you cannot communicate it to your people. The ultimate goal for all leaders is motivating and inspiring the people they serve. Great leaders deliver a message that is filled with optimism and hope. It is a message that makes others want to maximize their potential and be the very best they can be, no matter what they are doing. Motivating others to have the courage to exhibit a positive attitude, make the very best choices they can make daily, and to give 100-percent effort every day is the magic of every great leader. Super Freaks have incredible communication skills, and they have the ability to articulate their message in such a way that it paints a picture of the vision others can see and want to follow. Outstanding leaders communicate their vision with words and by being role models of each step toward its achievement, so that team members understand and become committed to the vision.

When I think of using the power of communicating in such a way that all who listen benefit and are playing and living at their best, there is no better feeling. Great communicators understand how people think and feel. They know that people want to feel special, and they sincerely compliment them by showing them respect and by communicating how highly each person is valued—as fellow employees, teammates, audiences, or clients. People seek direction, so outstanding leadership navigates for them. Communicating the vision means speaking to the needs of the people you serve and encouraging them every step of the way.

I often think about the first man to walk on the moon, Neil Armstrong, and how his message was communicated to the world. Can you imagine how motivating and inspiring it had to be for those first astronauts to look forward to venturing out into space? The words spoken on that day and at that moment were the words of an outstanding leader who had an incredible vision and certainly knew how to communicate it. As soon as his feet touched the moon, Apollo 11 astronaut Neil Armstrong's first words were, "That's one small step for man, one giant leap for mankind."

People Skills are another key component of outstanding leadership. To be a great and effective leader, you must know how to relate to and work with people effectively. People want to know that you care about them. For the most part, people are selfish, so as a leader you must always speak to their needs. You must recognize when they are low emotionally and encourage, inspire, and motivate them to soar to their highest heights. Having great People Skills means acknowledging that yes, it's true that we are all more alike than different, but it's our differences that make us unique. My grandfather used to say, "Son, treat everybody right, but don't you dare treat them all the same." In other words, each one of us is unique: Each person is inspired and motivated by different words and actions at different times. That simple little piece of advice has served me well over the years.

The Super Freak Way recognizes that great leaders make themselves visible and available to the people they serve. The open-door policy is in effect 24/7, and it is not just lip service. Outstanding leaders get to know the people they serve. Great leaders respect everyone and allow their hearts to get involved by always seeking the best in people and truly caring for them. Great teams have a better chance of winning consistently when their leaders know their people well. People skills include having empathy, compassion, and love for others and always being willing to lend a helping hand.

The fourth key to outstanding leadership is that great organizations and teams have men and women of character leading the way. *People of Character* maintain their integrity no matter the cost. Outstanding leaders model the way for others to follow. Staying true to the vision is by no means an easy task, but people of character commit to whatever it takes to do things right. Outstanding leaders ask no more from others than they would ask of themselves: They walk the talk daily. They are out in front—they *lead with their life*. To lead from the front, a great leader teaches others the ways to live and to achieve by walking the talk at all times. This type of leader does not tell others how to behave; instead, he demonstrates how to behave simply by being himself. He or she enjoys building bridges for others to cross. Great leaders always give more than they take. If you focus on what you can give to people rather than what you can get out of them, they will love and respect you.

Outstanding leaders can take any situation and make it into an opportunity for success. They simply do what they say they will do. In order for teamwork to grow within an organization, the organization must have leaders who are committed, consistent, and constantly making decisions that best benefit the people they serve. The Super Freak Way is always to lead with your life, serving others and creating a winning environment. Thomas Jefferson, the third U.S. president, summed up the character of an outstanding leader this way in a letter to his nephew, Peter Carr, in 1785: *"Whenever you are to do a thing, though it can never be known but to yourself, ask yourself how would you act, were all the world looking at you, and act accordingly."*

The fifth key component of outstanding leadership is that outstanding leaders are *Competent*. Being competent does not mean that you have all the answers or that you are a know-it-all. It means that as a leader, you utilize every resource to provide whatever your team needs to be successful, for example: necessary data, up-to-date equipment, coaching, tutoring, professional development opportunities, appropriate benefits, honest feedback, and one-on-one encouragement. Competent leaders are forever students. They are nonstop learners who embrace knowledge. Great leaders seek out every opportunity to learn and to share what they learn. Great leaders evaluate their strengths and seize opportunities to improve themselves.

They also seek out mentors, other successful leaders, to teach them how to improve their leadership skills by sharing their insights and experiences.

The Super Freak Way for learning is to know your craft. Become as proficient tactically and technically as you can. Put your whole self into being the best at whatever it is that you decide to do. When knowledge becomes wisdom, there is nothing more powerful. Wisdom is a by-product of taking theory and skillfully putting it in to action. At the end of the day, outstanding leaders are willing to roll up their sleeves and do the physical as well as the mental work. They always want to learn more than is required. We are never too old, too smart, or too wise to learn. Competent leaders are role models of successful performance because they work at learning how to be better daily.

Key component number six is that outstanding leaders are *Bold*. They are decisive when they make decisions. After analyzing how to solve a problem, they are willing to make a decision and stand by it. Great leaders constantly challenge themselves, are willing to change, and confront conflicts head-on. These qualities are key ingredients in our professional growth process. The more you grow as an individual, the more confident you become in your abilities to lead, communicate, and succeed. Great leaders keep their people informed, and they are bold enough to take the initiative and to praise their employees when they take the initiative.

To be bold is to be assertive. To succeed you will have to have the courage to go for what you want, to assert yourself. Assertive leaders hold themselves as well as everyone else accountable for accomplishing the group's agreed-upon results.

Being bold is more than giving a good speech. Boldness goes far beyond talking. Boldness is the physical and mental effort behind the words. It is doing the work every day and practicing what you preach. I like to say that being bold is setting your goal and achieving it: Set it and go get it!

Helen Keller was a normal baby until she was 18 months old, when a serious illness affected her brain, and she became blind and deaf. When Helen was 7 years old, Anne Sullivan, her lifelong teacher and friend, taught her sign language by tapping on her hand. Anne also taught Helen how to speak and write. She grew up to be an exceptionally bold, courageous woman who wrote books, gave speeches, and became a social and political activist. Helen Keller explained how useless it is to live our lives based on fear: *"Avoiding danger is no safer in the long run than outright exposure. The fearful are caught as often as the bold."* In other words, just go for it!

And finally, outstanding leadership ultimately means being a *Servant to Others*. Leaders help others be the best they can be. Outstanding leaders inspire and motivate others to maximize their potential. They foster an atmosphere that is full of optimism and hope. Great leaders lead with their lives and model the way for others to follow. Outstanding leaders serve the community as a whole, not just their own organizations. The Super Freak Way teaches us, "If everyone helped just one person, then no one would ever be without help" (Almon Gunter, author of this book). Our legacy lives through our deeds. We have the power to shape, inspire, and motivate future generations through our actions today. *Great leaders understand the value and power of giving back by serving others.*

Becoming an outstanding leader requires that you know yourself and become a nonstop learner. It requires that you seek out mentors for guidance and proper development as a leader. Outstanding leaders become students of how leadership works; they learn the causes of other leaders' successes and failures. Great leaders develop a genuine interest in people, set high goals, and plan wisely for reaching their desired destination.

Outstanding leadership is achieved when you become proficient technically and tactically in every aspect of what is expected of you, and you spend your time and energy mastering those skills. Proven leaders always want to learn more than is required of them to do their jobs. They spend time with a circle of colleagues and friends who are known for being organized, proficient, and the best at what they do. Outstanding leaders look forward to receiving feedback that can make them better, and they seek out opportunities to apply what they learn. They know that good leadership skills, in the end, are mastered through practice.

As a great leader, get to know the people you serve, and look out for their well-being. Be approachable and put the welfare of the people you serve before your own. Let them see that you are fully prepared to help them to achieve their goals successfully. Stay in touch with the attitudes and thoughts of your people, and ask for their opinions. Listen to them. The Super Freak Way tells us to treat everyone right, but not to treat everyone in exactly the same way. Find the catalyst for each person you serve, and then inspire each one in a different way. Keep them all informed and inspired.

Outstanding leaders model the way. They are willing to do everything that they ask of others. They maintain a positive attitude and are optimistic about the future. Leaders stop rumors by replacing them with the truth. They share their own and others' success stories throughout the organization, family, or team. Outstanding leaders lead from the front.

John Kenneth Galbraith, economist, author, and ambassador, said, "All great leaders have had one characteristic in common: It was the willingness to confront unequivocally the major anxiety of their people in their time. This, and not much else, is the essence of leadership." When great leaders see that their team members are fearful or anxious, these leaders tell the truth. They admit to their own fears and share their methods for controlling them. Great leaders help their players figure out the sources of their fear and show them how to overcome fear and anxiety.

Scribbles and Doodles

What has been the most valuable thing you have learned thus far and why?

_____
_____
_____
_____
_____
_____
_____
_____
_____
_____

List 3 things that you do to serve others and add value to their lives.

_____
_____
_____
_____
_____
_____
_____
_____
_____
_____
_____

How do you currently lead with your life?

_____
_____
_____
_____
_____
_____
_____
_____
_____
_____
_____
_____
_____

Final Thoughts:

_____
_____
_____
_____
_____
_____
_____
_____
_____
_____
_____
_____
_____

CHAPTER 3

Trust and Respect

Trust. As members of any team, we must trust and respect the people we work and play with. If you doubt that they will come through for you or be there for you when the going gets tough, you may as well pack it up and throw in the towel. Super Freaks trust and respect ourselves to deliver; therefore, we trust and respect others on our team to deliver as well. Trust and respect are built on facts, not emotion, so everyone can win.

As Ritu Ghatourey, a writer from India, says, "The most important elements of any relationship are trust and respect. When you trust someone enough to be honest with them, you grow to respect them and yourself. Where there is trust and respect, progress resides."

In any relationship, trust is needed for the relationship to develop and grow. Without trust, maximum effort or maximum progress will never be obtained because the lack of trust in others will keep individuals from giving 100 percent to the goals set for the team. The moment that any team member loses trust in another member (or members) is the moment the team is no longer a team playing for the same goals and objectives. When one or more individuals lose trust in any of the others, the team instantly becomes a group of individuals who are simply covering their own butts when the situation inevitably turns from bad to worse. When this happens, individuals start to make decisions based not on what's best for the team; instead, they make decisions based on what is best for them. Unfortunately, we witness this type of behavior in almost every walk of life. To succeed consistently as a team—whether a family, an organization, a business, or a sports team—every person must believe in and stay focused on one shared vision, one mission, one overall goal.

Trust is something that takes many weeks, months, and sometimes years to gain, but only a second to lose. In order to gain the trust of others, you must first trust yourself. As a leader, you must trust that you will make the best decisions for the team, not just at the right moment but at every moment. Trusting yourself to do what's best requires that you are *a servant of others*—whether you are the CEO, the most experienced veteran, the newest team member, or the head coach. You always treat people right—even if they cannot give you anything of benefit in return. In the end, you'll gain others' trust because they know you always do what you say you will do. They trust you because your actions and words are in complete alignment. At the moment you fail to do what you say you will do or your actions and words don't align, that is the moment others' trust in you begin to be broken. At that moment, doubt starts to creep in. And when doubt exists, your ability to succeed gets harder. Broken trust is usually followed by broken promises, dreams, and hearts.

Once trust has been broken, it is so hard to regain. For individuals who feel betrayed, losing trust in a family or team member can be paralyzing. Betrayed people can feel so hurt, so heartbroken, that they may find it difficult to open themselves up to love, sharing, and caring again. We all have experienced betrayal at one time or another, but the hard truth is that unless we regain the ability to be open to the art of possibilities (to trust others again), we spend the rest of our lives existing instead of living. Significant growth and inner strength can come from experiencing and overcoming adversity. Some of the greatest achievements in life can result from the necessity for self-preservation. When any type of adversity or betrayal occurs, great teams, families, and organizations possess the gift of sticking to the facts and not letting themselves get mired in the emotions of the situation. Sticking to the facts when we discuss problems or betrayals allows us to seek solutions for healing. Facts give us the first glimpse of what we need to do to create a roadmap for change. And through change, individuals and teams can find new ways to grow and become more cohesive.

Broken trust doesn't have to be the end to your dream. The Super Freak Way is to believe that you have the moxie and determination to get through whatever comes your way. It is so hard not to take broken trust personally, but if you let your emotions (such as hurt, anger, disgust, sadness, or disappointment) control your actions, chances are you will be miserable for a long time. You must maintain your ability to see the art of possibilities through the obstacles you encounter, for that is the key to bouncing back from a setback.

We all have the power to choose our behavior. When we have been knocked down and are feeling overwhelmed by negative emotions, we can choose to stay down, or we can choose to get up and make it a better day. As Super Freaks, we persevere (keep going) by doing our best work, by training as hard as ever, and by showing our love to our families and teammates. For teams to be successful, the members have to be willing to set aside their emotions (i.e., put them into a separate compartment of their minds) so they can think logically about the facts of the situation. Of course, we feel anger, hurt, and disappointment just as deeply as everyone else. The difference is that we Super Freaks have trained ourselves to think logically and to persevere no matter what happens. We are totally honest with ourselves as we analyze why we feel bad, and then we choose to turn that negative, wasted energy into positive energy so we can be open to change and growth. *The Super Freak Way is Xtreme Perseverance.*

Outstanding teams' members have no problem having the hard conversations with each other. They never lose sight of the team's vision, mission, or goal. They hold each other accountable to do what they say they will do. The leadership always presents a message that is clear, concise, constant, and consistent, so that team members are armed with substance—not fluff. I agree with the cliché "the truth hurts," but I also know if we give ourselves enough time and effort, we'll all start to heal and move on. Teams that trust each other love each other as teammates. They may not always agree on everything, and they may not like each other personally, but they do love the team and what the team as a whole represents.

Trust is built on a solid foundation of clear communication. When team members are open and willing to listen to each other, deep trust can be built throughout the team. When roles and responsibilities are clearly defined and when team members have the knowledge and skills needed to succeed, they will trust each other willingly. Our shared experiences also enhance our ability to trust team members. The more trust we gain and give, the deeper our levels of interaction and expressions as a team will be.

Respect. Respect is another key component of building an outstanding team. Respect starts with the man or woman in the mirror. Self-respect allows us to have compassion and to care for others. When we establish a positive, can-do relationship with ourselves, it transfers into every aspect of our lives. The Super Freak Way demonstrates that respect equals good behavior, and good behavior equals respect. So, in a nutshell, displaying self-respect and maintaining respect for others come down to choices we make.

Self-respect allows you to love the real you. You love who you are on the inside—not just for what you do for a living or how you look on the outside. When you are proud of who you are and know that you have value as a person, you are well on your way to having self-respect. The key is knowing how to take care of yourself first, while serving others in the process. If you constantly put others' needs before your own or continuously sacrifice your physical and emotional needs while serving others, this self-sacrificing behavior will become damaging to you, which amounts to not respecting yourself. It is a fine line we must navigate because the harsh reality is that we cannot attend to everyone else's needs by neglecting our own. Members of outstanding teams and businesses know how to attend to their own needs so they can better respect and serve the needs of their teammates and colleagues.

Members of outstanding teams choose to respect one another. They trust that every team member will do the right thing, not only at the right moment but every moment. Outstanding teams are built on trusting and respecting the leaders of the team, who set the tone for the rest of the team. Usually, the trust, respect, and morale of any team reflect its leadership. Great leadership plays a major role in creating a winning environment that is nonjudgmental and centered around trust and respect. This type of environment focuses on the here and now and encourages team members to make a difference today.

Trust and respect start with the leaders and then flow among all team members. When leaders demonstrate several key actions and attitudes, they will establish, promote, and maintain trust and respect throughout their organizations.

First, great leaders do what is right. As a supervisor or coach, you must be willing to do what is right regardless of the personal risks to you. For the most part, we all have a strong sense of what is right. Trust and respect yourself and your team enough to do the right things, and you will gain their respect. Ultimately, respect will lead to trust.

Second, consider all members of your team to be equal partners. When individuals feel they have value and matter to the goals of the team, they trust their leaders and teammates. Inclusion helps to build buy-in from everyone.

Third, establish and maintain integrity throughout the team. The foundation of trust and respect is integrity. Be true to your word, and do what you say you are going to do. In turn, your behavior will be reflected by your team members. Even when you must share information with your team that is not good, put it all on the table—tell the truth. Truth builds trust and respect among all members of the organization.

I learned this lesson about the importance of sharing the truth even when it's difficult or uncomfortable when I was working for an organization in the mid '90s. It was a great place to work, and if the company were still in existence, I would probably be working there today. The company wasn't doing well, and the leadership team delivered the message truthfully and professionally—that the company was going out of business. As a result of the honest presentation of that unpleasant message, I walked away with respect for the leadership team. Every so often, I run into people who worked with me at this organization, and we all talk about how great it was to work there and the friendships that were made and still exist today from working there.

Fourth, as a leader, communicate your vision of the team and the high value of all members often. Communicating your vision tells everyone which direction the team is headed, and communicating the values of the team establishes the road map for meeting team goals. Sharing trustworthy information with everyone will keep team members engaged in the winning process. Whenever you speak to team members, focus on using the word "we" instead of "I." Talk about the team's or organization's goals versus personal or individual goals. The essence of teamwork from the leader's point of view is ensuring that all members feel they are working together to accomplish one mission, one vision, and one goal.

Establishing and maintaining respect for yourself and for all the people who work with you allows members the greatest opportunities to make progress and grow exponentially toward reaching team goals. Mutual respect promotes collaboration, trust, and honest communication among team members. When people feel you value them as human beings, they are more inclined to trust, communicate, and work with you. In the long run, the more respect you give, the more respect you will receive. As a leader, you will see that being respectful is simply the right way to live.

"This world of ours must avoid becoming a community of dreadful fear and hate, and be, instead, a proud confederation of mutual trust and respect." Dwight D. Eisenhower, 34th U.S. president and five-star general in the U.S. Army

Scribbles and Doodles
How do you incorporate trust and respect into your daily life?
_____
_____
_____
_____
_____
_____
_____
_____
_____
_____
_____

List 3 things you do to create more trust and respect within your team, organization, and family.
_____
_____
_____
_____
_____
_____
_____
_____
_____
_____
_____
_____
_____

Why is self-respect so important to you and your team?

_____
_____
_____
_____
_____
_____
_____
_____
_____
_____

Final Thoughts:

_____
_____
_____
_____
_____
_____
_____
_____
_____
_____

CHAPTER 4

Outstanding Talent

O*utstanding Talent.* *When we evaluate teams that progress and win, it's clear that they are loaded with outstanding talent. Exceptional teams are not made up of a group of individual superstars; instead, they are made up of a group of individuals who work together as one unit for the same common cause.* Outstanding talent can be summed up as talent that is coachable. *Individuals who are coachable listen well and actually hear and execute what is said. They practice every day to be better. They welcome feedback and crave any information—including constructive criticism—that can help them to become better. Talented individuals are willing to do whatever it takes to get better for the team so team goals and objectives can be met. They set themselves apart by having the mentality of "repetition, repetition, repetition," practicing and perfecting their skills daily. This is the only way to win consistently.*

Talented individuals know that talent alone doesn't guarantee a win. The Super Freak Way stresses this fact: hard work will beat talent every time if talent doesn't do the hard work. Hard work is the key ingredient that will give talented teams the best chance of winning consistently. People with outstanding talent have an understanding of the game that they are playing mentally and physically at all times. They are willing to stay committed and focused on team goals. If an organization or team is going to succeed, it must recruit and nurture these types of individuals. Outstanding teams and organizations employ talented individuals who are dedicated to working hard to reach the organization's goals.

Talented people have a knack for putting themselves in the right position to win. They pay close attention to details and visualize the next move needed to succeed. Super Freaks stay constant and consistent in our approach to learning. We keep our minds open to the possibilities of each day because new opportunities for success come with each new day. The combination of talent and hard work leads to desired results.

When I look back, I recall playing with and against many athletes who were more talented than I was. Some were faster, stronger, quicker, and smarter, but I still had to find a way to compete. My parents and grandfather did an outstanding job of preparing me mentally on how to stay focused and how to be confident in my abilities in any situation or competition. We had regular conversations about staying the course, persevering, and never quitting—no matter what. They reminded me that just because someone was a little faster, stronger, or smarter than I was, it didn't mean I couldn't win. They taught me that success would always come down to working hard.

My parents and grandparents taught me that the person who concentrates on getting things right, never takes shortcuts, and has the heart, courage, and will to last through adversity will win. It didn't matter what the scoreboard showed when time ran out. What mattered most to me was knowing that I never took a play off and that I gave all I had to the goals and objectives of the team. This mentality is what takes ordinary talent and turns it into extraordinary talent. Having the heart and willingness to hustle every day helped me to develop the courage needed to stay on track and pursue my goals. When you give your best every day—every time you practice and every time you compete—there is no way you can lose.

These life lessons have served me well. I realize that I have achieved athletic and career successes that many would say were beyond my capabilities. But that is the beauty of sports, education, and life: At some point we all have to play the game. Life shows up regardless of who you are, so you can choose either to compete or to be a spectator. It doesn't matter where you were born, what your nationality is, what your socioeconomic situation is, or who your parents are—we all eventually get to write our own story.

For me, repetition and hard work have helped me continue to succeed. Sure, I have talent, but I know it has been my will to succeed, my tenacity to stay in the fight, and my ability to continue to do the heavy lifting day in and day out that have allowed me to learn, risk, and grow. I trust my own foundation, values instilled by my parents, grandparents, and people I respected in the community. I realize that not everyone is fortunate enough to have parents, grandparents, and community leaders like I had, people who shaped and developed my foundation. However, I often think of something my grandfather said to me on several occasions: "The library is full of role models." Reading is the key to being exposed to the many possibilities and opportunities that come with each day. Find someone you can identify with through the written word, your personal hero or heroine, and use that person's story to help you write your own success story.

I believe we all have some type of talent, but many of us don't recognize or develop our talent. We are too busy complaining, overvaluing what we don't have and undervaluing what we do have. Where you start in life is not as important as where you finish. So, get busy writing and living your own success story!

I do understand that recognizing and identifying your talent can be hard. I will be the first to admit that sometimes the quality you perceive to be your talent really isn't it at all. If you had asked me back in high school where my talent was, I would have said, "Football!" I really liked playing it. I loved everything about the game. However, my mother saw something different in me and guided me to my true strengths. She had a real concern that I would get injured playing college football, and her primary goal for me was that I would get a college education. She knew that academically I was prepared, but she also knew I had always been a student athlete, and the athletic part of my life kept me focused. The possibilities of my playing college basketball or running track made sense to her, so I opted for college track over basketball. Because of the respect and trust I had for her, I listened to what she had to say and was open to these new possibilities. (Okay, I really didn't have a choice because she only said things once!) Through my mother's genius, I would later discover that my passions and talents were in education (formal and informal) and in running really fast!

Once I started to place high value on what I had inside of me, my true passions and talents were revealed. You don't have to be a track athlete to know that running is hard. There are no easy running workouts! If you are competing in the 200 meters dash, you can't run 195 meters and call it good. You have to run 200 meters for it to count. It doesn't matter how well you practiced the week before or how good you feel leading up to the race. What matters most is how you performed at that moment, at that time on race day. Life works the same way. Sooner or later, you are going to have to show up and compete. At some point, life forces you to prove what you know and what you are made of. It exposes your heart, soul, and mind. In the game of life, you are either a participant or a spectator. You choose how you'll play the game.

We all have some type of outstanding talent. Everyone has the capacity to be exceptional in a given area. What prevents us from realizing our goals or from achieving our maximum abilities is our lack of will to practice. Yes, I am saying, "practice makes perfect." That is, perfect practice leads to perfect performance. The more you practice anything, the better you will become, especially if it is something that piques your interest. Think about it for a moment. Recall something that you wanted to learn, say, speak a new language, play a particular sport, or play a musical instrument. When you committed to practicing consistently, did you get better? The answer is probably 'yes.' I believe that outstanding talent is achieved through practice. It is achieved by working toward your goal every day.

Yes, there are some rare exceptions, like child prodigies who can play a piece of music after listening to it once, but the most examples of outstanding talent are achieved through practice. Michael Jordan will always be considered one of the greatest basketball players in the world (or maybe the greatest), but he wasn't born that way. His rise to the top of the basketball world is clearly documented. After getting cut from his high school varsity team as a sophomore, Jordan committed himself to becoming better. He didn't commit with words; he committed with actions. He practiced, practiced, practiced. The same can be said about Walt Disney, one of the most innovative geniuses of all time. Disney persevered in spite of several setbacks and seized opportunities for improvement. He dedicated his life to what he was passionate about—people. Both of these individuals practiced hard to overcome whatever obstacles were in their way to fulfill their destinies.

Of course, some activities and pursuits come easier to a few gifted people than to others, yet in the end, the most talented individuals are the ones who have worked the hardest.

Great teams thrive on people who are eager to learn and work at achieving the one mission, one goal, and one vision of the team. Successful teams lack egocentric members; instead, they are composed of individuals with more "we attitude" than "me attitude." Outstanding teams are built by individuals who never lose sight of the overall mission of the team—exceptional performance—and who are determined to stay the course, weathering any storms despite the pressures that come with success. Talented people are dialed in mentally and committed to the end.

Super Freaks know that life comes with change, so we are systemic thinkers. We anticipate how change in one area will affect another area. This view allows for solutions that are supportive and beneficial for the entire organization when changes occur. Individuals with outstanding talent involve others in their quest to reach team and individual goals. They are well aware that no one makes it to the top on his or her own. Successful individuals seek out mentors whose skills, experiences, and power sources support their efforts, such as experts in the field and knowledgeable colleagues. Super Freaks draw strength from diversity and are organized, rigorous, disciplined, and prudent. Truly talented individuals let the evidence of their work speak for itself. This, characteristic builds trust among their teammates and demonstrates their commitment to the team's goals and objectives. Talented people who work hard every day to improve are essential for any successful team.

"Talent without discipline is like an octopus on roller skates. There is plenty of movement, but you never know if it is going to be forward, backwards, or sideways." H. Jackson Brown, Jr., author of *Life's Little Instruction Book*

Scribbles and Doodles

Have you identified your talent? (If so, what is it? If not, what are you waiting on?)

_____
_____
_____
_____
_____
_____
_____
_____
_____
_____
_____
_____

List three things that make you coachable.

_____
_____
_____
_____
_____
_____
_____
_____
_____
_____
_____
_____

How do you allow others to help with your quest to meet team and individual goals?

_____
_____
_____
_____
_____
_____
_____
_____
_____
_____
_____
_____

Final Thoughts:

_____
_____
_____
_____
_____
_____
_____
_____
_____
_____
_____
_____

CHAPTER 5

Committed

***C**ommitted.* Teams that win are committed to each other. Great teams are in it for the long haul. They see the big picture, and they work toward it every day. Committed teams don't confuse the amount of time spent pursuing and achieving a goal with the quality of time pursuing and achieving a goal. For example, you hear individuals talking about how they arrive at work early and stay late because they are committed to the organization, but the reality is many of those individuals are balancing their checkbooks or surfing the Internet. Time wasted is not quality time. Commitment involves more than showing up. Commitment is actually doing work that improves your performance and benefits the team once you show up.

The Super Freak Way regarding commitment is centered around the quality of time spent. Are you spending your time doing the things needed to make yourself and the team better? Are you utilizing your strengths and working diligently to follow up on opportunities for improvement? Are you doing what you *say you will do daily?* These are the questions that must be answered with a resounding, "Yes, I am!" day after day after day.

Committed individuals and teams believe wholeheartedly that failure is not an option. All other options except for creating success have been cut off. As long as there are options or fallback positions, there can be no real commitment. Think about it: When you have a safety net or you know that if plan A doesn't work out, you will just go to plan B, you will not be all-in. For example, I am pretty sure at some point we all have experienced the following scenarios: (1) Have you ever been in that tough spot when you had a project deadline for a class or in your organization, and if you didn't meet it, the consequences were going to be extreme? (2) Your instructor, supervisor, or parents told you to complete a task, and if it wasn't completed, life as you knew it was not going to be fun? Chances are, whatever the project or task was, you got it done, right? Now my questions are, 'Why did you get it done? Why were you able to deliver in a big way at that particular moment?'

The answer is probably that the consequences for not getting it done were greater than your pride or your butt could stand! Your mental capacity to face the consequences of failure was something you feared you might not be able to overcome. Failure was not an option for you. You refused to be defeated or come up short in completing your task. For the Super Freak, this is commitment.

We accomplish what we set our minds on. And when we absolutely, positively have to deliver in a big way, we focus our time, energy, and strengths on hitting the mark. The best position to play from is with your back against the wall because that position doesn't allow anything to get behind you. Everything has to come toward you. You develop a laser-like focus. Individuals and teams that are committed focus on keeping things in front of them. They work and compete with the heart and attitude that make every moment an important moment. No time, no motion, and no energy are wasted. All their work is high quality with a desired result in mind.

Staying committed to do what you say you are going to do is no easy thing. This is what we Super Freaks call "Walking the talk." Achieving some of our smallest goals is hard because of the tedious tasks that must be performed daily to ensure success. Commitment is not a goal—it is a mentality. It is a state of mind that Super Freaks live with every day: XTreme Perseverance. Successful people's commitment to being the best is tested daily by staying the course even when no one is watching.

I remember the days of going to the track alone to do the workouts my coach had scheduled for me. (There are no easy track workouts.) And let's say my workout was to run 300 meters six times at 35 seconds each time. After running the fourth 300, I was exhausted and looking around, saying to myself, "Maybe I won't do the last two." Or, "Okay, I will run the last two but not as fast and just try to get through them. After all, I am all alone on the track, so who will know?" These thoughts were constantly running through my head. Well, the truth is that I ran those last two just as fast as the first four because I would know, and I couldn't live with myself if I'd slacked off. Plus, I realized that on race day everyone watching would know whether I put in the work. So, in the end, I found a way to keep breaking through the mental and physical barriers of pain to do what I said I would do. I believe every successful person lives his or her life this way. We all have a threshold of pain or tolerance, and once we learn to push beyond it, there is nothing we cannot achieve.

Organizations that succeed and teams that win are made up of individuals who work hard even when no one is watching. They never have to make adjustments in their level of effort because they always give the best they have. I have found that giving your best every day, is the best, most satisfying way to live. When I worked in a corporate environment, there were times when the president or senior vice president from the home office was visiting, and everyone would get nervous. Managers would run around and tell everyone to look busy and stay focused. I would think to myself, "Isn't that what we should be doing every day?!" Giving our best effort daily should not be negotiable.

Commitment isn't a part-time gig. There can be no gray areas in commitment. You are either committed, or you are not. Unfortunately, many individuals like to choose when they are committed, but this philosophy will only produce inconsistent results. My grandfather had a story for this type of behavior. He would say, "Real commitment is being like the pig. When you eat eggs and bacon, the chicken participates, but the pig is committed." It didn't matter if the pig went voluntarily or was forced; in the end, all other options were cut off, and the pig was committed.

Successful teams commit to a specific goal, which is crucial when chasing success. Without a specific goal to play for, the team may develop bad habits, procrastinate, or become lazy. In other words, mediocrity starts to set in. Teams that win have individuals who not only know the definition of sacrifice, but they actually put the word into action. Agreeing to work hard for the team is different from committing to work hard for the team. When we make an agreement to do something, we have options. We can keep the agreement, cancel the agreement, or change the agreement. When we commit to something, we keep our commitment no matter what. When we make a commitment, whatever we are committing to is easier to obtain. Commitment takes time, effort, and self-discipline. Our self-discipline grows out of a commitment to our goals. Commitment allows our choices to become clearer, creating a "do whatever it takes" mentality.

Having a "do whatever it takes" mentality does not mean backstabbing or belittling others to get what you want. Instead, it does mean making that extra phone call, staying a little later if necessary, or doing one more thing to assure progress and success even when you don't feel like it. Great teams create a winning environment that makes it easier to do that one more thing, to persevere until we achieve our individual and team goals.

Making the connections among our values, our intentions, and our actions is true commitment. It is surrendering our whole selves to a goal. When you are committed, you are willing to do anything positive to support that commitment. Commitment drives us, and during our most challenging times, it is our commitment that serves as our anchor. It helps us to maintain our integrity as we work toward the common goal. Commitments are choices we all get to make at some points in our lives. Our commitments become our self-expressions, like street signs saying who we are and how we have chosen to live as individuals. I believe that our commitments are what allow us to live out our personal best!

Vince Lombardi, the head coach of the Green Bay Packers who led the team to five NFL championships, had this to say about commitment: "The quality of a person's life is in direct proportion to their commitment to excellence, regardless of their chosen field of endeavor."

We all can be great if we utilize our strengths and never stop learning, risking, and growing as individuals. More important, we must maintain our courage and will to succeed at all costs to ourselves.

Scribbles and Doodles

Name one team goal you are committed to achieving in the next three months and why.

_____
_____
_____
_____
_____
_____
_____
_____
_____
_____

List three personal qualities that allow you to maintain your commitment to your individual and your team's or organization's goals.

_____
_____
_____
_____
_____
_____
_____
_____
_____
_____
_____

How do you maintain a connection among your values, intentions, and actions?
___
___
___
___
___
___
___
___
___
___
___

Final Thoughts:
___
___
___
___
___
___
___
___
___
___
___

CHAPTER 6

Passionate

Passionate. *Teams that win consistently are made up of individuals who are passionate about what they do. Not only are they passionate about winning, but they are passionate about the game they are playing and passionate about the well-being of the members of their team. Winning will seldom occur if team members are not passionate about what they are playing for. It is difficult to give freely of ourselves every day to an organization or a person that our hearts aren't into.*

Being passionate about who you are and what you are doing requires that you approach life with enthusiasm. You must approach every day with a zest for life that is second to none. When you have enthusiasm, what you are revealing to the world is 'I Am Sold Myself.' The last four letters of the word "enthus**iasm**" say it all—**I A**m **S**old **M**yself—I am totally committed to what I'm passionate about. The Super Freak Way encourages all people to be sold themselves. After all, if you are not sold yourself on something that is important to you, how are you going to sell it to others or convince others to support it? The greatest thing about passion is when it is present, everyone can see and feel it. Passion is what puts fire in our bellies and allows us to be a part of something that is bigger than ourselves. Passion gives us a spark for life, and, in turn, that gives us more life to share with others.

For many of us, discovering the one profession or artistic endeavor or purpose that drives us can be difficult, but I think we all have that one special thing inside of us that makes us smile from the inside out. So how do find your passion? A great place to start is to seek the answers to the following questions:

> What is that one thing that you think about every night before you go to bed?
> What is the first thing you think about in the morning that makes you want to jump out of bed to accomplish it?
> What is the one thing that gives you the will to keep going when everything around you seems to be going wrong?
> What is the one thing that drives you to give all you have and not settle for giving less than your best?

When you can answer these questions clearly and concisely, chances are you will discover your passion. You will discover the blueprint for your purpose in life.

Another way to discover your passion is to ask yourself, "What would I do as a career if I didn't have to worry about how much money I make? If you could do anything in the world with no worries of providing for yourself and your family, what would it be? Would you choose the career path that you are on right now, or would you choose a different path? Interviews with the some of the most financially successful people of all time suggest that if you follow your passion, success and income will follow. The common thread for these successful people was that their passions played key roles in their successes. The late Steve Jobs, co-founder and CEO of Apple Inc., said that people should do what they love doing. He said that what drove him was his passion for his work and a belief that "people with passion can change the world for the better."

Chris Gardner, the once homeless man who turned himself into a multimillionaire stockbroker, philanthropist, and author, played by Will Smith in the movie *The Pursuit of Happyness*, expressed what he believes is the secret to success: The secret to success is to "find something you love to do so much, you can't wait for the sun to rise to do it all over again." Gardner says that the most inspiring leaders are those who don't feel like they're working at a job but are pursuing a calling.

Warren Buffett, investor, philanthropist, and one of the wealthiest people in the world, knows that there is more to success than money. In a 2008 article, "10 Ways to Get Rich: Warren Buffett's Secrets That Can Work for You," number 10 says,

"Know what success really means. Success is different for each of us. Find what it is that brings meaning to your life, what makes each day important. Make this your focus. When you get to my age, you'll measure your success in life by how many of the people you want to have love you actually do love you. That's the ultimate test of how you've lived your life" (To see all 10 of Buffett's secrets, go to an article by J. D. Roth at www.getrichslowly.org/blog/2008/09/10/warren-buffetts-ten-secrets-to-wealth-and-life).

We all need to discover what brings true meaning and passion into our lives and make that activity or profession the focus of our lives.

I absolutely love what I do! Every day I get to live out my purpose of helping others, as well as myself, to maximize the potential we all have. I often say I am a nerd who just happens to be athletic. This combination gives me an incredible outlook on life. My sister constantly reminds me that I don't have a real job because she says all I do is write books, talk to groups, and help people get physically and mentally fit. So, she refers to me as "Kramer" from Seinfield. She says no one knows what Kramer does. I laugh because she is absolutely right in so many ways. My mission is pretty simple every day: to be the best I can be for the day, serve others, and have fun doing it! I eventually discovered my passion, what matters to me the most, by looking back at my childhood. I thought about the things that made me happy as a child. I loved school, so education was definitely at the top. I loved participating in sports—competing and working as a team player—so fitness was an obvious choice. And, I loved feeling needed and loved by my family and friends, so helping and serving others was a no-brainer.

Then I took a look at the people I thought were successful. I asked myself questions: How did they get there? What did they do differently from others? How did they overcome obstacles? I didn't try to complicate things or reinvent the wheel. My goal always was and is to learn from the best. My grandfather reminded me that there are plenty of successful people to learn from in the library. So, I read about them and learned how to grow. I visualized what it was that I wanted and wrote those goals down to remind me of what I was playing for. Once I allowed myself to be open to the possibilities of creating what I wanted, I went for it. I didn't have all of the answers. I risked failure in order to succeed, and I am so thankful that I did.

The Super Freak Way
I decided to call the combinations of my passions in life "The Super Freak Way." The Super Freak Way came into being because I was always sports-minded and enjoyed school and learning. When an athlete performs at an incredible level, he or she is often referred to as a "freak of nature." The same is said about individuals who are academically gifted. The older I got, the stronger I became and the faster I ran. Mentally and physically, I was different. So, my family and friends referred to me as a "freak." They didn't call me a freak to be mean or to put me down; from them, this name was a compliment. I realized the combination of mental and physical fitness really work hand in hand. (By the way, super heroes and heroines are smart individuals who somehow end up with some mental or physical super power. Just saying!) As I researched successful people in business, sports, and other professions, the one thing they had in common was that they never quit. They found a way to get through the hard stuff—no matter what the cost was to themselves. I learned that Super Freaks blaze paths for others and risk failing in order to succeed.

If you want to become a Super Freak, you must be truly passionate about the work you are doing, and you'll have the greatest chance of achieving success. When we are passionate about something, we work a little harder, we dig a little deeper, we stay a little longer, and we inspire everyone who works beside us. Great teams are made up of people who don't consider what they do "work" because they love what they do. We are happiest when we are doing what we love every day, and that, my friend, is success.

Success is more than being famous or making a lot of money. Success should be defined as "an achievement of something desired." So, when you really stop to think about it, successful people are the ones who achieve the things they desire. In many ways, doing what you love to do, what you feel compelled to do, or living out your calling is so much better than working only to gain fame or wealth. Chances are, if you are doing what you love, you will be great at it and will get paid accordingly. Successful people who do what they love seem to end up financially, mentally, and spiritually in a better place than most. Finding your passion may not be easy to do, but discovering it is well worth the time and effort.

Super Freaks know that it is never too late to discover your potential or to find your passion. If you have already discovered your passion and you are pursuing it, you should give yourself a big pat on the back because you, my friend, are in the minority. The Conference Board Job Satisfaction Survey of 2013 says, "For the seventh straight year, less than half of U.S. workers are satisfied with their jobs" (https://hcexchange.conference-board.org/blog/post.cfm?post=1927). In 2010, the same survey's report said that most people were working for their current employer because "they felt they had to." Doesn't that sound sad and dull? Is that how you want to live your life? Of course not!

Unless you were born with unlimited resources, not working isn't an option. However, even if you aren't happy with your job and can't quit now, you can still pursue your dream. There are 24 hours in a day, so set aside a time each day to go after what you want—talk to experts in the field and ask for their advice (most people love to give advice), do research on the Internet, and/or offer to do volunteer work for an organization or an individual whose work you admire. Sometimes we do what we have to do so we can eventually do what we want to do. Find a way to make the transition from where you are to where you want to be. *It is never too late to become who you want to be and to pursue your passion.* You just have to be willing to make the commitment, sacrifice some free time, and have the courage to move forward.

Earl Nightingale, radio commentator, author, and personal development pioneer, said,

"The only person who succeeds is the person who is progressively realizing a worthy ideal. He or she is the person who says, 'I'm going to become this' and then begins to work toward that goal" (To listen to Nightingale's presentation, "The Strangest Secret," go to www.youtube.com/watch?v=GakfEmYBukQ).

Successful people and successful teams channel their intense desire and enthusiasm to get to where they want to be. They focus their passion and stay the course. We all have a purpose in life, and it is imperative that we seek out our purpose and live it to the fullest. At some point, we need to look in the mirror and ask theses questions, "Why am I here? What am I supposed to do with my life?" Write down the thoughts that come to your mind when you ask yourself these questions. The answers will come to you.

As I've continued to dig deeper into learning about passionate individuals and teams, I've realized that they are not discouraged by obstacles or setbacks. Though they may feel discouraged for a little while, they don't give up. Actually, they use their frustrations and being outside of their comfort zones to push themselves to compete at higher levels. They also use the fire inside of them for what they want to accomplish to help them to develop whatever it takes to succeed mentally. Passionate people also understand that it's natural for all of us to have fears. They accept that their own fears of failure, hard work, insufficient time, and not pleasing other people can all be turned around to keys for success.

And another important point: Passionate teams and individuals are resilient. When they fail, they do not quit. They keep their eyes and minds locked onto their goals. Their never-quit attitude gives them the energy to bounce back from disappointments and setbacks. Ultimately, passionate people are able to live out their passions because they patiently work toward their goals and put up with discomforts, rejections, and delays so they can follow their hearts to experience true fulfillment.

In her best-selling first book, *A Return to Love: Reflections on the Principles of "A Course in Miracles"* (1992), Marianne Williamson, spiritual activist, lecturer, author, and founder of The Peace Alliance, said,

> Our deepest fear is not that we are inadequate.
> Our deepest fear is that we are powerful beyond measure.
> It is our light, not our darkness,

That most frightens us.

We ask ourselves
Who am I to be brilliant, gorgeous, talented, fabulous?
Actually, who are you not to be?
You are a child of God.

Your playing small
Does not serve the world.
There's nothing enlightened about shrinking
So that other people won't feel insecure around you.

We are all meant to shine,
As children do.
We were born to make manifest
The glory of God that is within us.

It's not just in some of us;
It's in everyone.

And as we let our own light shine,
We unconsciously give other people permission to do the same.
As we're liberated from our own fear,
Our presence automatically liberates others.

Along the same lines, I want to share with you a few words from the awesome late Nelson Mandela—a man who always 'walked the talk' and lived his life passionately with extreme resilience. He spent 27 years in prison as punishment for political activism against apartheid, won the Nobel Peace Prize, and became South Africa's first democratically elected president.

In *Long Walk to Freedom: Autobiography of Nelson Mandela* (1994), he wrote,

I am fundamentally an optimist. Whether that comes from nature or nurture, I cannot say. Part of being optimistic is keeping one's head pointed toward the sun, one's feet moving forward. There were many dark moments when my faith in humanity was sorely tested, but I would not and could not give myself up to despair. That way lays defeat and death.

And here are his words excerpted from an interview he gave in 1994 for the documentary film *Mandela*:

The greatest glory in living lies not in never falling, but in rising every time we fall. . . . Do not judge me by my successes; judge me by how many times I fell down and got back up again. . . . After climbing a great hill, one only finds that there are many more hills to climb. . . . I learned that courage was not the absence of fear, but the triumph over it. . . .

Scribbles and Doodles
Have you discovered your passion? (Why or why not?)

_____
_____
_____
_____
_____
_____
_____
_____
_____
_____
_____
_____

List 3 qualities you have that can contribute to your success:

_____
_____
_____
_____
_____
_____
_____
_____
_____
_____
_____
_____

Do you create the world in which you want to live every day? (How? Why or why not?)

_____
_____
_____
_____
_____
_____
_____
_____
_____
_____
_____
_____

Final Thoughts:

_____
_____
_____
_____
_____
_____
_____
_____
_____
_____
_____
_____

CHAPTER 7

Empower Each Other

Empowering others *is easier said than done. 'Empower' can be defined in two ways. One definition, from a legalistic viewpoint, is to give a person the authority to do something. A second definition is to enable someone to do something, to give that person more opportunities for independent action, making him or her stronger and more confident. Super Freaks tend to go with the second definition and take it a little further, viewing the word empower as simply 'to let go.' Outstanding leaders have learned that the most effective way to empower others is to enable individuals to make their own choices. In this way, the individuals who report to us are responsible for the consequences of their choices.*

Successful teams encourage all team members to execute their roles. *These organizations hire the best-qualified people to use their individual talents to benefit the entire team. The coaches of outstanding teams empower all team members. When we are empowered to make our own choices in our jobs,* teams, and families, we are motivated to do our very best. We are confident in ourselves because our supervisors or coaches have enough faith in us to let us go, to let us make our own choices.

Every member of a business or a team is there for a reason and serves an important purpose. They have specific roles to play, and they bring certain skill sets or gifts that can benefit the team. When you look for a job, you may send in your résumé, be interviewed, and/or audition by demonstrating your skills. You'll be asked to discuss and perhaps demonstrate the unique skills and experiences that make you qualified to perform the job well. Essentially, you are showing that you can meet and exceed all the requirements to help make the organization or team more successful. You are agreeing to help this group of people further pursue its vision, mission, and goals as an organization.

Successful teams enable all team members to do best what they say they can do. The organization's leaders assure that each team member has the resources needed to be successful, and then the leaders move out of the way to allow all members to stretch their wings and fly. When baby eagles' wings have grown enough for them to fly, their mothers bring meat near the nest to coax them to come out, grab the food, and start to fly on their own. If an eaglet falls to the ground, its mother will feed it until the eaglet figures out how to fly. In similar ways, leaders of great teams, support and empower their members to succeed. At some point, we all have to be 'let go' to test our wings. Successful teams thrive when all members of the team learn, risk, grow, support, and encourage each other.

We cannot excel or reach our full potential while we have a safety net. As long as we are being micromanaged or allowed to give excuses for not doing our best, we will only become a mere fraction of who we are supposed to be. We are all diamonds (believe it!), and diamonds are created by applying pressure. Through the adversities in our lives, the mistakes and wrong choices, we react in one of two ways—we either SHRINK or GROW! Learning to be comfortable with being uncomfortable and staying the course no matter what happens are keys to reaching your maximum potential.

Empowering others to be their best, in my opinion, is one of the most unselfish actions you can accomplish in life. I believe we owe it to each other to push and encourage one another to fulfill our destinies. As parents, it is so hard to let go of our children. We spend our lives trying to comfort them and keep them safe from harm. We tell ourselves that we are protecting them when we try to shelter them from broken hearts, disappointments, and frustration, but we are dimming their lights. As a parent, I know at some point my children will have to compete. I have come to realize that if you are a parent, your parenting skills will be tested. Your leadership skills, vision for your child, and how you have communicated that vision will be put on the table. You will have to let your children risk being the very best that they can be. You will eventually have to let go or end up raising what my good friend the late Dr. David B. Langston would refer to as "old children." These are children who never test their wings and stay in the nest forever.

Leaders who empower their teams not only help the people they lead to grow; they help themselves to grow as well. If your hands are full because you are trying to micromanage and do everything yourself, you can't pick up anything else. The only way you can grab on to something else that may help you and your teammates to improve and meet goals is to let go of them and empty your hands. As a leader, you must trust that all team members understand their roles and have the ability to execute their roles to perfection. This is where 'leading with your life' shows up. *When leaders model the behaviors and values they are trying to establish in their organizations, others will get on board.* When leaders walk the talk, they build good organizations into great ones.

As adults and leaders, it is critical that we model the behaviors we expect to see from our children and colleagues. I have learned that when you celebrate the things that you want to see more of and stop rewarding mediocrity, individuals exceed our expectations. Sometimes it is hard as a parent or as a leader to risk establishing boundaries for our children or the people we are leading because we may fear not being loved or liked. We must remind ourselves that leadership is teaching, supporting, and stretching others to maximize their potential. It is helping individuals to tap into their God-given talents to be all that they should be. As a leader and a parent, I have found, that when I love or care for individuals enough to risk losing them—because I won't settle for mediocrity from them or myself, I end up gaining their respect. At these times, they may not like you, but they will respect you, and in most cases, they will learn and never forget these lessons.

To empower others is the greatest compliment you can give. It says to people that you truly believe in them, that you trust in them and their ability to get the job done. It says you know that they are not only capable of doing the right thing, but that they will do the right thing at the right time regardless of the circumstances. *My mother, Eunice Gunter, would often say, "I will never say what my children will not do. I will only say what I hope they will not do. I know, good is in them because I put it there."*

Now that I am older, I have come to realize and confirm what I already knew: my mother is an amazing leader. She has always modeled the behavior she wanted from my siblings and I, and she never wavered on teaching us that right was right. On the front end, she was willing to risk us not liking her because of her tough love in order for us to respect, love, and adore her on the back end. However, today I sit and watch her with the grandchildren, and I wonder, "Who is this woman?!" I point out to my children that this is not the same woman who raised me. This is a kinder, gentler mom. And then my mom smiles and says, "I don't have to be tough on them because you are doing just great at that job!" And then it hits me: she is right. She taught me how to lead my children, so now she gets to move on and grow in different ways. She is a genius!

Successful teams have outstanding leadership that empower them by providing the resources and tools needed to teach every team member how to do the job right. No egos, no jealousy, or taking short cuts for success are involved. There is only vision: hard work, talent, and constant communication. Teams that win consistently have leaders who compliment team members for a job well done. They are grateful and appreciative of the sacrifices made by each team member to meet and exceed team goals. Outstanding leadership knows that one pat on the back for a team member will bring far more benefits than a hundred kicks in the butt. It is all too easy to focus on the negative things that happen and forget about the many positive things that occur every day. Successful teams have leaders who praise in public and reprimand in private.

Teams that empower each other send messages of trust and respect. All team members feel they have value as individuals and add value to the team, that they play critical roles in the team's overall success. When you have buy-in from each member on a team, it is easier to get where you are going as a whole. We all want to know what's in it for us if we do our part. That is human nature. So, it is important as a leader to make sure that every person on your team knows that the work that he or she does is not in vain. Great teams from top to bottom and from bottom to top express and show gratitude and appreciation for one another.

When we make the choice to let go and let others do what they do best, so we can do what we do best, everyone benefits. We all have what it takes to shine brightly on the inside and on the outside. *Minister, author, television and radio commentator Joyce Meyer says, "You can be pitiful or powerful, but you can't be both at the same time."*

Scribbles and Doodles
Do you feel you are empowered? (Why or why not?)

_____
_____
_____
_____
_____
_____
_____
_____
_____
_____

List 3 ways you empower members on your team. (Family, work, school, teammates)

_____
_____
_____
_____
_____
_____
_____
_____
_____
_____
_____
_____

What is your best example of empowerment? Either empowering others or experiencing being empowered yourself:

_____
_____
_____
_____
_____
_____
_____
_____
_____
_____

Final Thoughts:

_____
_____
_____
_____
_____
_____
_____
_____
_____
_____

CHAPTER 8

Think Team

Successful teams 'think team' always. I know this seems like it would be an obvious fact, but it certainly is not. In today's world, it is so hard to be a team player or to think team constantly. In our culture of instant gratification, we have created an 'all-about-me' generation. Social technologies, such as Facebook, Twitter, Instagram, and others, can be useful tools to stay in touch with old and new friends. Instead, what they seem to promote is an all-about-me mentality. Every post, every message, and every photo seem to scream, 'Look at what I did!'

In contrast with the all-about-me mentality, the Super Freak Way promotes the wolf philosophy: The pack is the wolf, and the wolf is the pack. *Being a dedicated member of one unit moving in the same direction for the same cause is the only way to win consistently.* Successful teams possess this spirit of togetherness from top to bottom. All individuals in the organization feel that they are essential, that their talents contribute to the overall success of the team. Teams that win have members who understand that if there was an 'I' in team, it would stand for *i*ndividual effort toward achieving the common goal. As a team, you have nothing if every individual isn't giving the very best effort that he or she possibly can for the sake of the team—not for his or her on personal glorification.

I have raised my children with the philosophy that together we can move mountains, but only if we work together. No one becomes successful on his or her own. There is always someone who gave a hand up—not a handout. Mike Krzyzewski (Coach K), head basketball coach at Duke University and head coach of the U.S. men's national basketball team, gives his team a great talk each season. He holds up his hand and displays his five fingers. He points out that this is the number of players who are on the floor for each team, but when the hand is open, it is not a very powerful punching tool. You can hit someone with the open hand, and it will hurt but not as bad as it would if you brought your fingers together and made a fist. When you come together and make a fist, now you have a very strong instrument to punch with. Then he goes on to explain if one finger becomes an individual, the fist starts to lose its effectiveness as a punch. So, it is important to stay together and work as a team. Coach K's philosophy is, "We win as a team, and we lose as a team."

Depending on others for the success of the team means everyone must trust and respect everyone else's abilities. When the going gets tough, team members must demonstrate the courage to rely on their training and to rely on each other. To think team, you must have the ability to communicate using the words 'we,' 'us,' and 'our' at all times because this is the only way to promote the one-team mentality.

As a track and field athlete, I had the pleasure of experiencing teamwork in a way that gave me an incredible perspective. Track and field taught me that I was the team, and the team was me. There are roughly 22 different events in track and field. The events are broken down into five different categories: sprinting, middle distance running, long distance running, jumping, and throwing. Depending on the size of the meet, points are awarded to finishes 1 through 8. The team that scores the most points when all 22 events are completed wins the track meet. So, sprinters weren't necessarily best friends with distance runners (after all, we sprinters can't seem to figure out why anyone would want to run for miles), but all of us cheered for our teammates. We cheered because we understood that their efforts and contributions provided valuable points that the team needed to be successful. Track and field are where I truly learned that the 'I' in team stood for individual effort. It was each athlete's individual effort that determined how well the team would do when the final scores were tallied. So, we all learned to work together and to inspire and encourage each other in any way we could to benefit the team. I have managed to use this philosophy in every aspect of my life.

When we learn to think team, we learn to sacrifice ourselves when necessary to benefit the team. We are willing to give in ways that many can't imagine because we are playing for something that is much bigger than ourselves. We give up the individual accolades for team championships. I bet if you were to ask Hall of Fame basketball great Charles Barkley or Hall of Fame football great Dan Marino if they would give up all of the individual statistics and honors for a world championship ring, they both would say, "Yes!" In the end, we recognize, publicize, and even criticize great teams.

These same principles apply to all successful organizations. The following quotation is often attributed to Henry Ford, founder of the Ford Motor Company:

"Coming together is a beginning. Keeping together is progress. Staying together is success."

Think Like a Team

To think like a team, here are eight requirements you and your teammates or coworkers can follow:

Team Attitude Requirement No. 1: Be Unselfish.
"You've got to totally get out of yourself and into the unity of the team." Pat Riley, professional basketball executive and former coach of championship teams

"Having a TEAM ATTITUDE calls for an alignment away from a 'me and my' position into a 'we and our' position." Almon Gunter, author of this book; motivational speaker and consultant; speed, strength, and conditioning coach

Team Attitude Requirement No. 2: Find a Role and Fill It.
"Creating a successful team is essentially a spiritual act. It requires the individual involved to surrender his self-interest for the greater good so that the whole adds up to more than the sum of its parts." Phil Jackson, professional basketball executive and former coach, author

Team Attitude Requirement No. 3: Be a Team of Cheerleaders!
Encouragement promotes growth.
Praise enhances morale.
Commendations increase cooperation.
Carping and criticism kill your fighting spirit.

Team Attitude Requirement No 4: Follow the Leader.
Be sure that the roles of the leader and each member of the team are clearly defined. Develop a high value and respect for every member of the team.

Great leaders model the behaviors they expect their team members to follow.

"The winning WE attitude starts at the top of the organization." Pete Rose, former professional baseball player and manager, author

Team Attitude Requirement No 5: Be Flexible.
The official motto of the Marine Corps is *Semper fidelis*, meaning "Always faithful." The unofficial motto is *Semper gumby*, which means "Always flexible."

Great team leaders and members show the following attitudes and capabilities:
Adaptable
Creative
Coachable
Eager to try new ideas and new approaches
Not rigid or stuck in a rut

To be flexible and adaptable, we have to accept changes and unforeseen circumstances.

"You've got to adapt to every new situation, condition, and contingency. Sure, we've all got to fill our own roles—but when circumstances change, we've got to change, too." Pat Williams, motivational speaker, professional basketball executive

Team Attitude Requirement No. 6: Have Fun!
Avoid using pressure tactics to motivate people.
Avoid using fear to motivate people.
Be instrumental in making work a fun experience.

Each one of these successful individuals—Terry Bradshaw, Fred Shero, Bill Veeck, and Michael Jordan—has made this statement:
   "Learn to have fun out there!"

Are you having fun? Whether you are one of the newest members of your organization, a CEO, a coach, a veteran team player, or the company's public relations director, ask yourself this question: Are you having fun? If so, great! If not, take some time to figure out what your passion truly is, and do whatever it takes to go for it!

Here's some important advice from me to you:

"Stay loose, babe. Whatever game you're playing, whether you play it on an athletic field, in an office, on the road, or in a church, enjoy the heck out of that game. Have a blast! Have fun out there!" Almon Gunter

Throughout this book, we have been working on how to build a team attitude. If you follow these recommendations, you will become more effective in building your personal life and your professional life.

The last two guidelines, numbers 7 and 8, are those of Coach Pat Williams, a professional basketball executive and author of many books. He has written several books about Coach John Wooden, who is, Williams says, "the greatest coach who ever lived." Wooden's teams won 10 NCAA championships in a 12-year period. When Williams asked Wooden to name "just one secret of success in life," Wooden answered, "The closest I can come to one secret of success is this: a lot of little things done well." Williams relates this conversation in the Introduction to one of his recent books, titled *Wooden's Greatest Secret: The Power of a Lot of Little Things Done Well* (2014).

Williams makes the following points in an earlier book on how to build winning teams.

Team Attitude Requirement No 7: Think in Sync
To think in sync, think in harmony by
Working together,
Being unselfish, and
Encouraging every other person on the team.
Learn to maintain your unity while celebrating the diversity and uniqueness of each individual.

Team Attitude Requirement No 8: Give Yourself Up
Give yourself up for the good of the whole by setting aside enough time to work as hard as you can for the team or organization. Train and practice new techniques, and get to know each other.
(Williams, 1997, *The Magic of Team Work: Proven Principles for Building a Winning Team*)

When we allow ourselves to think in terms of what is best for the team, everybody wins. 'Thinking team' means that you believe in the cause of the team. It says you are willing to give and do whatever is necessary to help your team meet and exceed its goals. Allow yourself to imagine for just one moment what the world would be like if we all thought and played in terms of 'we' instead of 'me.' If that happened, the world's people would have all the help they would ever need all the time. Helping others to be the best that they can be is the Super Freak Way!

Scribbles and Doodles

How do you bring value to your team?

_____
_____
_____
_____
_____
_____
_____
_____
_____
_____
_____
_____

List five things that you do to Think Team.

_____
_____
_____
_____
_____
_____
_____
_____
_____
_____
_____
_____
_____

Do you have a team attitude, behavior, and effort? (Why or why not?)

_____
_____
_____
_____
_____
_____
_____
_____
_____
_____
_____
_____
_____

Final Thoughts:
_____
_____
_____
_____
_____
_____
_____
_____
_____
_____
_____
_____
_____

SUMMARY

Teamwork is often spoken of but is rarely understood. It is one of those things that everyone likes to talk about because it sounds so good. The concept of teamwork is great, and people like to feel they are doing their part to help their team win. However, the reality is very few people live and play as though every day is game day.

Great teams are first and foremost built with **People of Character**. People of character simply do what they say they will do. They stand by their choices, and they hold themselves and others accountable for staying on task. In order for any team to be great, it is essential that all the people on the team have strong personal values, creating the right foundation for the whole team. With the right foundation, any team can grow to be anything it wants. The stronger the character of each team member is, the stronger the team's foundation.

Teamwork requires **Outstanding Leadership** that leads with their life. Outstanding leaders blaze a trail for others to follow, while making sure that the people they lead have the resources they need to achieve their own goals and the team's goals. Outstanding leaders treat everyone right, but they don't treat everyone the same because they recognize that we are all unique in our own ways. Teams that win consistently have leaders who are visionaries. These leaders constantly model the behaviors they would like to see from their people every day on the job. Great leaders communicate their vision in such a way that everyone buys into the dream.

Trust and Respect are key cornerstones in the essence of teamwork. Without trust and respect among team members, winning will be hard to do. Great teams foster an environment of trust and respect. They strive to make sure that each team member knows that he or she is valuable and that each person plays a key role in the overall success of the team. The Super Freak Way encourages team members to stick to the facts when communicating and chasing team goals. Facts allow for clear, concise communication, free of emotion that may distract individuals from what the message should be about. Teams that keep it simple when it comes to trust and respect give themselves a greater chance to meet and exceed team goals.

Great teams have **Outstanding Talent**. Individuals who possess outstanding talent are coachable. They listen well and pay close attention to details; even more importantly, they have a positive, can-do attitude. Talented people are always trying to learn. They yearn to be better, and they put forth the effort daily to be the best that they can be. People with outstanding talent always stay in the moment. Successful teams have individuals who understand that repetition and hard work are the only ways to learn, risk, and grow. Talent may get you invited to the big dance, but it's the hard work, repetition, attitude, and effort that allow you to execute the right steps at the right time under all circumstances.

The Super Freak Way describes **Commitment** as the quality of time spent doing whatever it takes to hit your goals, versus the amount of time you spend pursuing your goals. Commitment is more than showing up. Commitment is doing the work once you get there. All members of the team must do whatever they can do to the best of their ability for the team to be successful. No one whines, no one brags, and no one criticizes another teammate's work. Commitment requires a group of individuals to work together to achieve excellence for the organization. Commitment doesn't rely on words, but on actions!

Members of great teams are **Passionate** about what they do. Passionate people love what they do for a living and are highly motivated. Successful teams are filled with motivated individuals. When we are passionate about what we do, we feel that our work has value. Organizations that create one vision, one goal, and one mission through outstanding leadership, clear communication, and strong commitment contain passionate individuals who never take a play off.

When teamwork is at its best, individuals **Empower Each Other**. Leaders empower team members by providing resources, being concerned for the people they lead, and building bridges for others to cross. Outstanding leaders let go and allow team members to do what they say they can do. Teams that promote empowerment among team members will always have the greatest opportunities for growth and success.

Successful teams always **Think Team**. Each team member thinks and acts in terms of 'we' instead of 'me.' They act upon what 'we' can do to be better as a whole. Teams that think team play with the right attitudes, right behaviors, and maximum efforts daily. Everyone is truly All-In, and each team member never takes a play off or gets distracted from the task at hand. In the end, when we think team first, we can never lose.

The Essence of Teamwork means:

Having the courage to risk being great within yourself even if you fail.

Being empowered to take a chance and step outside of yourself even when you are uncertain.

Cheering each other on and wishing each other the best.

Feeling passionate enough about your work that you are willing to sacrifice what you must without resentment because you are doing what you love.

Serving others as an outstanding leader and as a dedicated team member.

Teams that walk-in hope and faith have no need to fear. Fear paralyzes us and takes away our creativity. Team members who have hope in each other and encourage each other will never lose faith. Adversity can teach us just how powerful we really are. Being down is not the end, but staying down makes it harder to get up. So, get up one more time than you are knocked down, maintain hope and faith in yourself and others, and miracles will come into your life.

The Essence of Teamwork . . . courage, risk, growth, sacrifice, commitment, passion, encouragement, empowerment, teamwork, hope, faith, and miracles!

Scribbles and Doodles

When it comes to your team do you walk the talk of a 'we' attitude or a 'me' attitude? (Please explain)

_____
_____
_____
_____
_____
_____
_____
_____
_____
_____

List five things that you can do to be a better teammate daily.

_____
_____
_____
_____
_____
_____
_____
_____
_____
_____
_____

What does *The Essence of Teamwork* mean to you on your current team?

_____
_____
_____
_____
_____
_____
_____
_____
_____
_____
_____
_____

Final Thoughts:

_____
_____
_____
_____
_____
_____
_____
_____
_____
_____
_____
_____
_____
_____

ABOUT THE AUTHOR

Almon Gunter is an expert when it comes to inspiring individuals to find the desire, dedication, and determination they need, to succeed in achieving their goals. His formula for success involves nonstop enthusiasm, hard work, and heart and hustle—with the end result of becoming an MVP in the game of life.

Gunter is the CEO/President of AGE 3, LLC. He is a highly acclaimed motivational and inspirational public speaker, author, and consultant. He competed as a world-class sprinter in US Track and Field. He uses his experiences on the track and as a business executive to help inspire others in the game of life.

Gunter is a Life Coach who focuses on mental and physical fitness. He believes that all people have goals. He asks the individuals he coaches what their goals are from day one. Gunter believes that all people can achieve anything they set their minds to and helps them believe that the tools for achieving these goals are within themselves. His role is to help every individual find his or her tools for success and refine them into razor-sharp instruments. Once these tools are refined, all individuals will have the self-confidence to succeed and win—no matter what they choose to do.

Acknowledgements

Special thanks to my children. Just as a bundle of sticks tightly tied together cannot be broken, we cannot be broken as a family when we work together as a team. Choose the road less traveled—as American poet Robert Frost's poem "The Road Not Taken" says—and that will make "all the difference" (www.poetryfoundation.org/poem/173536). Blaze new trails. Don't be afraid to build bridges, knowing that some of the bridges you build will not be for you to cross but for others to cross. Great leaders serve others.

To the world's greatest mom, Eunice Gunter, thanks for building a strong foundation within me. You are and will forever be my rock! And to my Aunt Edna Brown, thank you for looking after mom and making it easier for me to rest at night, knowing she is in good hands with you by her side. To my siblings, I love you dearly. We have it all because we have each other.

Dennis Webber, I honor and respect you as a friend, mentor, leader, and trusted advisor. Your words of encouragement daily keep me focused and driven; I truly appreciate all that you do. A great big thank you to my dear friend and colleague, Eric Bass, for writing an incredible Foreword for this book. Bassman, I can always count on you to deliver. Thanks to the Nickerson family (Nick, Judi, Trey, and Jordan); as a family, you are the essence of teamwork! To my friends the Formoso's (Ferdinand, Elisa, Alex, Nick, and Teddy P), you all certainly keep me motivated and inspired. Thanks for your support and encouragement.

As always, a sincere thanks to my wonderful brothers from another mother, Windle (Peck) and Earriet (Easy), for being there for me no matter what. You two have always been in my corner, pushing me forward. I appreciate you both. Also, thank you to Ricky Battle, who is always there with an encouraging word. And to Tommy Sampson, you bigggg . . . you know I love you to life, brother! To my dear friend Cassandra Jenkins (CJ), you are always there reminding me that we all have the power to do great things. Go Noles! Bruce Canady, please know that your friendship is appreciated daily. Shelda Moll (Shell Bell), thank you for simply being you. You have an incredible heart and spirit; don't ever change.

There are many others who helped me along the way, and I say thank you. No one achieves success alone, and I am grateful for all the help I receive from so many on a daily basis. I am grateful for your love, and I will continue to learn, risk, and grow through *The Essence of Teamwork*!

For more information
on other products by
Almon W. Gunter, Jr.
KEYNOTE
BOOKS
TRAINING CAMPS
CONSULTING
Please contact
AGE 3, LLC
Post Office Box 194
Jacksonville, FL 32234
Phone: 904.803.1917

Website: www.almongunterexperience.com
Email: almon@almongunterexperience.com
Twitter: @almongunter
Facebook: Almon Gunter Experience
LinkedIn: Almon Gunter
Instagram: Almon Gunter Experience
YouTube: Almon Gunter Experience
Podcast: Almon Gunter Experience
TikTok: @almongunterexperience

Give AGE 3 a call today
so you can live The Super Freak *Way* and Focus To Win!

www.ingramcontent.com/pod-product-compliance
Lightning Source LLC
LaVergne TN
LVHW051954060526
838201LV00059B/3644